AuthorHouse™
1663 Liberty Drive
Bloomington, IN 47403
www.authorhouse.com
Phone: 1-800-839-8640

First published by AuthorHouse 03/05/2012

ISBN: 978-1-4678-6993-5 (sc)

Library of Congress Control Number: 2011960202

Printed in the United States of America

authorHOUSE®

COMPILATION BY NICA PERSONNA & CO. 2011

FOREWORD

In a world full of hungry people searching for answers, Nica Personna presents WOW. If there was ever a time people needed to understand the fruit of the spirit is now.

The presentation and revelation of this book will give all who read it the nine foundational building blocks to build on their dream. WOW is a must read and I highly recommend it!

- Bishop Wallace Duane Swilley

ACKNOWLEDGEMENTS

I want to thank the One who chose me long before I came on the scene for this assignment. Father God I thank you for Your faithfulness, yes indeed, GREAT IS THY FAITHFULNESS. Thank You for Your ordered steps, the corrections, and Your mercies in my life.

Constance (Connie) Roberty, I thank God for you and your parents Myrtho and Frantz Roberty because without you this project would probably still be just that, 'a project'. You are a very intelligent young lady who has so much to offer this world, and that is why your battles are what they are. You are a child of the Most High and the victory is yours.

Dominique Routier, my encourager and supporter in all my endeavors. Thank you Dom, for being willing to always answer my calls, even at the last minute, which is usually when I call on you. I thank God for the wonderful gifts that He has placed in you and which have made this book possible.

I thank God for my families at A Place Called Hope. To my family at House Of The Living God, thank you. To my Hope prayer group and Destined Prosperity Group, thank you for your guidance. A very special thanks to Mrs. Rosalind Lassiter-Roker of The Roker Resource Group and Seon George for your leadership.

To my instructors at Life Christian University, it is amazing how true the saying is 'little is much when God is in it'. How wonderful, to think that a simple assignment could turn into this. Better yet, how God can show up anywhere in the least expected places, such as while cleaning the children's room in the church. Yes there is favor in the cleaning ministry!

To Cynthia Rider for introducing me to Continental Societies Inc., thank you. Thank you to my sisters at the North Dade Broward County Chapter. Mrs. Shirley Williams thank you for that advice years ago when you called on me to do the devotions, for 'in life you have to be always ready '.

Thank you to Maryline Routier and Ralph Belizaire for their assistance. Finally to Sean Burke, thank you for being the anchor in this project. You have great talents that must not be taken lightly. God loves to honor those who honor Him.

Thank you Holy Spirit.

INTRODUCTION

Many times God will ask us to do something that will result, in the natural, as a great loss but in the spiritual realm, great gain. Words Of Wonder is the result for such an obedience. The Lord knew that I had a desire to do a book. He provided everything else, **EVERYTHING!** *Pastor Josh Swilley once stated that "we have the ability to create our world with our words. We take dominion with our words". We have all been given a gift, His Words. Go ahead, use them, because in them lies the power that you seek to accomplish your divine purpose on this earth. That is where your happiness lies.* **Live in the promise.**

"May the Lord give you increase more and more

you and your children.

May you be blessed by the Lord

who made heaven and earth."

- (Psalm 115:14-15)

REFERENCES

Biblical verses are from the **New King James Version**

Photos not by Stockphoto are by Evelyn Paniagua

Light up the sky with his spirit.

Allumez le ciel avec son esprit.

Iluminan el cielo con su espíritu.

Love

…by love serve one another …

…par la charité serviteurs les uns des autres…

…sino servios por amor los unos a los otros…

Joy

Do not sorrow for the joy of the Lord is your strength.

Ne vous affligez pas car la joie de l'Éternel sera votre force.

No os entristezcais, porque el gozo de Jehova es vuestra fuerza.

Nehemiah 8:10

Peace

Blessed are the peacemakers…

Heureux ce qui procurent la paix…

Bienaventurados los pacificadores…

Matthew 5:9

Patience

…let patience have its perfect work, that you may be perfect and complete…

…Mais il faut que la patience accomplisse parfaitement son oeuvre, afin que vous soyez parfaits et accomplis, sans faillir en rien.

…mas tenga la paciencia su obra completa, para que seais perfectos y cabales, sin que os falte cosa alguna…

James 1:4

Kindness

…what is desired in man is kindness…

Ce qui fait le charme d'un homme, c'est sa bonté…

… contentamiento es a los hombres hacer misericordia…

Proverbs 19:22

Goodness

Surely goodness and mercy shall follow me all the days of my life, and I will dwell in the house of the Lord forever.

Oui, le bonheur et la grâce m'accompagneront tout les jours de ma vie, et j'habiterai dans la maison de l'Éternel jusqu'à la fin de mes jours.

Ciertamente el bien y la misericordia me seguiran todos los dias de mi vida, y en la casa de Jehova morare por largos dias.

Psalm 23:6

Faithfulness

Nica Personna

For the Lord preserves the faithful…

…L' Éternel garde les fidèles…

A los fieles guarda Jehova…

Gentleness

A soft answer turns away wrath…

Une reponse douce calme la fureur…

La blanda respuesta quita la ira…

Proverbs 15:1

Self Control

Take control of what I say, o Lord, and guard my lips.

Éternel mets une garde à ma bouche, veille sur la porte de mes lèvres.

Pon guarda a mi boca, oh Jehova; guarda la puerta de mis labios.

Psalm 141:3

Most High God

It is by this fruit that all will know we are the children of the Most High God.

Il est par ce fruit que tout connaîtra que nous sommes les enfants de Dieu le plus haut.

Es por esta fruta que conocerán a todos los que somos los hijos del Dios altissimo.

Let your fruit be his light.

Laissez votre fruit être sa lumière.

Deje que su fruto sea su luz.

In an imperfect World where everything is constantly breaking down, we need tools to help repair them. When you find a tool that helps improve the condition of the dysfunction it makes you say "WOW."

Overcoming life challenges can be quite perplexing and God-given tools help us from being defeated. Finding a tool that helps improve the condition of the dysfunction can give you a "WOW" experience.

As we travel life's journey most experiences are not warfare, but a little tweak with the right tools will provide us a "WOW" experience.

Nica Personna has put together a toolbox with 9 essential God-given tools which will assist us in achieving a "WOW "experience.

This book will help you overcome your daily challenges.

- Pastors Clarence & Carol Brownlee

As a college student, the desires of the flesh are ever prominent among universities, dorm life, and just day to day interactions with others. To be given a direct outline as to the standard by which Christ calls us to walk by is a great accountability tool for me. Paul clearly lists the fruit of the Spirit, leaving no room for the lack of knowledge on how to face just about any situation. Everything is summed up in his list. For me at times, I see it as a lot to live by and the difficulty sometimes in following it, because as humans, sinful by nature, we are flesh-driven beings. However, Paul gives encouragement in his following verse stating, "And those who belong to Christ Jesus have crucified the flesh with its passions and desires." (v. 24). This verse reaffirms my identity in Christ as well as gives me the encouragement that I can walk by the fruit of Spirit because in me dwells the Holy Spirit.

At the close of the chapter Paul tells us that as Christians our passions and desires have been crucified with Christ and that we should walk in lock-step with the Spirit. Does this mean that we will no longer give in to temptations? That ought to be our goal, but the reality is that we are flesh, and despite our best intentions, we will continue to commit acts of the flesh. But the Spirit of God will guide all those who yearn to be free of sin towards sanctification and the blood of Christ will blot out the transgression of those who truly repent.

- Gerard and Valerie Nozea

I believe that the life of the believer is marked by the fruits of the Spirit. You can't help it! Once you truly invite Christ to be Lord in your life, His Spirit transforms the inner man. These fruits of love, joy, peace, forbearance, kindness, goodness, faithfulness, gentleness and self-control are a natural out-pouring of the converted life in Christ. Not that we are perfect, by any means. He Himself is the author and perfecter of our faith and He is absolutely faithful!

God wants us to cultivate the fruits of the Spirit although he knows we are sinners. All of them gravitate around one principal which is "Love". We are asked to love one another without expecting anything in return... To love the way God wants us to is one of the commandments.

- Daphnee Boulin Daniel

The Holy Spirit guides us in all truth and we are guided by the Holy Spirit. We walk in the fruit of the spirit. When we are led by the spirit, we demonstrate the love of God through goodness, gentleness, self-control, joy, peace, patience, kindness. When we act on this love, we realize that we are no longer our own - we no longer act in our own flesh, but rather walk in the Spirit, because we are a new creation in Christ.

- Donna Scott

When I think of the fruits of the Spirit, I think that Christ thought to leave us a blueprint for success on earth. If we walk in love, it is not hard to walk in gentleness, joy, peace, love, self-control, patience, kindness, and goodness. Do you ever think how wonderful life would be - even with all its difficulties - if all people strived each day to walk in the fruits of the spirit? How much kinder, joyful, peaceful, and gentler this planet would be simply by us walking in all of the manifestations of the true love of God. I do believe that was his plan for us!

- Dominique Routier

If you do not see the fruit of the Spirit in your life you do not have Christ living in you. Christ living in you will naturally be expressed in love, joy, peace, longsuffering, gentleness, goodness, faith, meekness and temperance."

- Dr. Eve Gualtieri, Director, Life Christian University, Miami Campus.

After reading chapter 5 in Galatians, I noticed that Paul was focusing on key facts. Paul tells us that we must use the fruit of the spirit to help us go through our everyday lives and be right with God. Paul states that the fruit of the spirit is love, joy, peace, longsuffering, kindness, goodness, faithfulness, gentleness and self-control. By applying these things to our lives, we are able to use them to eliminate the things that are against God's plan for us.

- Specialist Personna, Ricardo

It is a very good book because it gives people good advice of what words mean. When reading you can see the true meaning of Love, Joy, Peace, Patience, Kindness, Goodness, Faithfulness, Gentleness, and Self Control within the pages. Within all these words, you find God.

Fruit Of The Spirit

3 Things

1) Fruit grows. They grow slowly over a lifetime

2) The kind of fruit, which grows on the outside, is a reflection of the nature of the tree. The nature in you expresses itself in the kind of fruit that grows on the outside.

3) Fruits need fertilizer. God teaches one how to love.

- Rebelee (Christy) Jeyasingh RN MSN

The precious Holy Spirit, God's gift to us all. A gift we know cost the giver something but is free to the recipients. A lesson learned is obedience and love for our neighbor. In spite of the anticipated suffering, Jesus recognized the significance of His absence, the emptiness His disciples would experience after His death, therefore He prepared them as stated in John 14 that He will ask the Father to send another Helper, Comforter, Counselor, Intercessor, an Advocate, Strengthener and Stand-by who will be with us forever.

How wonderful and exhilarating to realize with confidence that you are never alone. God gave us a free will therefore the recipient can choose to cherish the gift and use it wisely, joyfully, with thanksgiving to the Father and the Lord Jesus.

- Celeste Lambert, Financial Advisor

This is a good story. It gives peace to someone going through something.

- Theodora Roberty

We are "juicy-fruits" living like the Holy Spirit". We are in good company fellowshipping with the Holy Spirit.

- Seon and Gail George

Printed in the United States
by Baker & Taylor Publisher Services